INVESTING IN AMERICA'S FUTURE

CHALLENGES AND OPPORTUNITIES FOR PUBLIC SECTOR ECONOMIC POLICIES

A STATEMENT BY THE RESEARCH AND
POLICY COMMITTEE OF THE
COMMITTEE FOR ECONOMIC DEVELOPMENT

Library of Congress Cataloging-in-Publication Data

Committee for Economic Development. Research and
        Policy Committee.
        Investing in America's future.

1. United States--Economic conditions--1981-
2. United States--Economic policy--1981-
3   United States--Social policy--1980-
I. Title.
HC106.8.C65 1988   338.973   88-22164
ISBN 0-87186-0 88-0 (pbk.)

First printing in bound-book form: 1988
Printed in the United States of America
Cover design: Stead Young & Rowe Inc.

PRICE: $9.50   89-35 50

COMMITTEE FOR ECONOMIC DEVELOPMENT
477 Madison Avenue, New York, NY 10022 / (212) 688-2063
1700 K Street, N.W., Washington, DC 20006 / (202) 296-5860

INVESTING IN AMERICA'S FUTURE

CHALLENGES AND OPPORTUNITIES FOR PUBLIC SECTOR ECONOMIC POLICIES

A STATEMENT BY THE RESEARCH AND
POLICY COMMITTEE OF THE
COMMITTEE FOR ECONOMIC DEVELOPMENT

INVESTING IN AMERICA'S FUTURE

CHALLENGES AND OPPORTUNITIES FOR PUBLIC SECTOR ECONOMIC POLICIES

CONTENTS

RESPONSIBILITY FOR CED STATEMENTS ON NATIONAL POLICY

The Committee for Economic Development is an independent research and educational organization of over two hundred business executives and educators. CED is nonprofit, nonpartisan, and nonpolitical. Its purpose is to propose policies that will help to bring about steady economic growth at high employment and reasonably stable prices, increase productivity and living standards, provide greater and more equal opportunity for every citizen, and improve the quality of life for all. A more complete description of CED appears on page 39.

All CED policy recommendations must have the approval of trustees on the Research and Policy Committee. This committee is directed under the bylaws to "initiate studies into the principles of business policy and of public policy which will foster the full contribution by industry and commerce to the attainment and maintenance" of the objectives stated above. The bylaws emphasize that "all research is to be thoroughly objective in character, and the approach in each instance is to be from the standpoint of the general welfare and not from that of any special political or economic group." The committee is aided by a Research Advisory Board of leading social scientists and by a small permanent professional staff.

The Research and Policy Committee does not attempt to pass judgment on any pending specific legislative proposals; its purpose is to urge careful consideration of the objectives set forth in this statement and of the best means of accomplishing those objectives.

Each statement is preceded by extensive discussions, meetings, and exchange of memoranda. The research is undertaken by a subcommittee, assisted by advisors chosen for their competence in the field under study. The members and advisors of the subcommittee that prepared this statement are listed on page vi.

The full Research and Policy Committee participates in the drafting of recommendations. Likewise, the trustees on the drafting subcommittee vote to approve or disapprove a policy statement, and they share with the Research and Policy Committee the privilege of submitting individual comments for publication, as noted on page 37 of this statement.

Except for the members of the Research and Policy Committee and the responsible subcommittee, the recommendations presented herein are not necessarily endorsed by other trustees or by the advisors, contributors, staff members, or others associated with CED.

CED RESEARCH AND POLICY COMMITTEE

v

FOREWORD

WHERE CED STANDS

This statement presents CED's perspective on what we believe are the most critical economic problems facing the nation and what we think should be done about them. Investing in America's Future differs from other CED policy statements in that it is an updated distillation of conclusions and recommendations drawn from recent in-depth CED studies of current issues.

It is intended as a guide for all individuals and organizations interested in sorting out the crucial economic issues affecting the health of this nation. It indicates clearly where CED stands on the major economic issues that have emerged in the current political campaign.

In the course of political campaigns, issues can become clouded and economic priorities confused. Therefore, it is critical not to lose sight of the fundamental public issues that have to be dealt with no matter what the electoral outcome. The sooner candidates and the voters focus on these issues, the more effective the political process will be in dealing with them.

The special value of this statement is that it offers policy makers and citizens an integrated approach to key national economic issues. Drawing on over a dozen CED studies, it succinctly outlines what we believe are the economic issues most in need of public action.

While Investing in America's Future summarizes the analysis contained in the source statements, the documentation presented here is not meant to be complete or comprehensive. The full research and reasoning that supports CED's policy positions can be found in the statements that have formed the basis of this report. These source statements include:

Toll of the Twin Deficits, 1987

Finance and Third World Economic Growth, 1987

United States-Japan Trade Relations: A Critical Juncture, 1987

Work and Change: Labor Market Adjustment Policies in a Competitive World, 1987

Children in Need: Investment Strategies for the Educationally Disadvantaged, 1987

Reforming Health Care: A Market Prescription, 1987

Leadership for Dynamic State Economies, 1986

Tax Reform for a Productive Economy, 1985

Investing in Our Children: Business and the Public Schools, 1985

Fighting Federal Deficits: The Time for Hard Choices, 1984

Strategy for U.S. Industrial Competitiveness, 1984

Productivity Policy: Key to the Nation's Economic Future, 1983

Strengthening the Federal Budget Process: A Requirement for Effective Fiscal Control, 1983

Public-Private Partnership: An Opportunity for Urban Communities, 1982

Jobs for the Hard-to-Employ: New Directions for a Public-Private Partnership, 1978

ACKNOWLEDGEMENTS

I would like to thank the members of the CED Program Committee who, along with other trustees, provided the leadership necessary to establish these priorities and set these goals. Very special thanks should also go to William F. May, former chairman of the Research and Policy Committee, under whose chairmanship this statement was prepared.

We are also deeply indebted to William J. Beeman, CED's vice president and director of macroeconomic studies and project director for Investing in America's Future, for his enlightened and insightful approach to these very difficult issues.

We also gratefully acknowledge the Ameritech Foundation and the CIGNA Corporation for their generous support which has permitted CED to expand substantially distribution of this important statement.

Dean P. Phypers
Chairman
Research and Policy Committee

Chapter 1

INTRODUCTION

Mixed signals are flashing for the U.S. economy. We have enjoyed the benefits of the longest-running expansion in the post-World War II era, several years of reduced inflation, and a high level of employment. We now have the opportunity to enjoy even greater prosperity in the future if the makers of public policy have the resolve to adopt and carry out certain basic economic reforms that can ensure major long-run benefits to our society. If we do not take this opportunity, however, our future economic progress and our nation's leadership position in the world may be threatened.

The most obvious economic challenges facing U.S. policy makers today are the federal budget deficit, the huge trade deficit, and weak growth in productivity relative to many other advanced industrial countries. But there are several other endemic problems that should be addressed, including a growing underclass of poorly educated and socially troubled individuals, disappointing educational quality in the public schools, and the gap between the promise and the delivery of adequate and affordable health care. These are tough and basic problems, and although many have already received some attention, progress to date has been far from adequate.

There is a tendency to look for a single specific overriding cause for these economic problems, be it an American society that is living beyond its means, unfair trade practices by our foreign competitors, or a decline in the American work ethic. Yet, in reality, both the causes of these problems and the actions needed to correct them are numerous, interrelated, and complex. Nevertheless, the solutions are achievable providing we develop the will to forgo some immediate consumption and invest more heavily in human and physical capital in order to encourage future economic growth.

This statement presents CED's perspective on the most important economic problems facing the nation, concentrating on those that can be addressed through public policy actions. We recognize that several other important issues that policy makers need to address promptly, such as the problems of drugs, crime, and housing, are not covered. We have confined our comments to the top-priority economic and social concerns that CED has been studying for several years; progress toward their solution will also provide resources needed to tackle other critical issues.

The conclusions presented in this statement draw from recent CED research on a wide range of issues. CED's Trustees have developed a body of recommendations designed to improve the fundamental health of the U.S. economy and to help policy makers rethink strategies in a new global context.

The policy decisions that we make as a nation in the next several years will determine the course that this country takes well into the next century. Economic policy decisions need to focus more clearly on the long-run benefits for society. They also need to reflect a much clearer understanding that the nation is functioning in an increasingly global economy. If we fail to adjust to the changes in the world around us, we simply will not take those actions necessary to provide for continued growth, prosperity, and an increasing standard of living.

The incoming Administration and Congress should view their first months in office as an opportunity to assess the challenges facing the nation and to break free of the rigid partisanship that is handicapping effective action. The United States can neither effectively deal with its economic problems nor retain its world leadership unless it musters the political will to put its economic house in order.

This can be done if policy makers begin now to take the following actions:

- Identify Critical Problems. In this statement, we identify the most pressing economic problems facing the nation and single out those areas of economic policy in which prompt, well-designed public-sector action is most critical.

- Set Priorities. In our view, the three most important objectives of economic policy today should be: (1) to significantly reduce our budget and trade deficits; (2) to improve productivity growth; and (3) to avoid protectionist policies in international trade both here and abroad. Achieving these basic goals will set the stage for reforms in many other policy areas.

- Assess Solutions. In deciding on courses of action, we need to capitalize on this nation's strengths. Free market solutions should be encouraged wherever possible, and public policy prescriptions should promote investment in the future health of the economy, even when this requires sacrifices. Finally, all actions need to be evaluated in light of the fact that the United States is now inextricably a part of a global, interdependent economy.

This statement proposes ways to deal with both short-term and long-term economic problems. Some of the proposed actions could achieve significant benefits in the near future, perhaps in one to five years. Our recommendation to eliminate the structural budget deficit, for example, would raise national saving, lower capital costs, and improve competitiveness fairly quickly. Other recommendations, especially those involving increased investment in human and physical capital, will take many years to bear fruit. But it is urgent that we act now to improve both the short- and long-run performance of the economy.

Chapter 2 outlines the broader signs of economic distress, including budget and trade imbalances and the macroeconomic causes of lost competitiveness. We recommend a budget policy of both reduced spending and increased revenues, and we outline how monetary policy can facilitate changes in budget policies.

Chapters 3 and 4 deal with the issue of longer-term economic growth. To enhance productivity growth we recommend specific policies in the areas of taxation, technology, regulation, and trade as well as policies to improve human resources in the areas of education, employment, health, retirement, and public welfare.

Chapter 5 addresses the importance of improving, strengthening, and streamlining the public institutions in which decisions are made, and the critical importance of the economic policies of state and local governments. In Chapter 6 we stress the overriding importance of building a constituency and a consensus for action. Practical bipartisan economic progress will come only if the Administration and Congress work out their differences in order to develop and support sound, practical economic programs. Such action needs to be motivated and backed by strong, vocal, and enduring public support. The American public needs to make it very clear that it will support those policy makers who will make the hard choices and follow through with their decisions. Once made, these decisions will bring real benefits. We believe that proper actions taken within the next year will bring the United States increased productivity growth, improved international competitiveness, and an improved quality of life.

4

Chapter 2

<u>BUDGET AND TRADE DEFICITS</u>

During the 1970s, growth in productivity slowed in the United States and inflation accelerated, reaching a postwar peak at the end of the decade. To counter these adverse economic trends, the thrust of monetary and fiscal policies was dramatically changed in the early 1980s. The Federal Reserve adopted a restrictive monetary policy for a time, and shortly thereafter, federal fiscal policy became very expansive. Federal spending grew rapidly and was accompanied by successive reductions in income taxes. Although monetary policy successfully reduced inflation, fiscal policy failed to achieve its objectives for domestic saving and investment and gave rise to very costly budget and trade deficits.[1]

The decline in the international competitiveness of U.S. industry was so dramatic that in a very few years, the United States went from being the world's largest creditor to the nation with the largest foreign debt. (See "Budget Deficits and U.S. Competitiveness," page 5.)

The huge successive federal budget deficits and the rapid growth in our debt to foreigners have encouraged and sustained the current cyclical economic expansion. But they also have two adverse consequences. First, they place a burden on future generations who will have to service both debts. Future payments of interest and principal to foreigners are particularly burdensome because they will transfer purchasing power abroad. Second, the budget and trade deficits create an increasingly unstable current economic situation both for our country and for the world because of our dependence on foreign saving. We can increase our debt to foreigners so long as we can service it and foreign investors desire to hold more of our debt. But, if foreign investors should seek to reverse these capital inflows, the consequence could be serious for the U.S. economy. Indeed, in 1987, private foreign investors began to lose confidence in the economic policies of the United States, and capital inflows from these sources fell, contributing to the sharp decline in the value of the dollar in international exchange markets. Large-scale intervention in foreign exchange markets by U.S. and foreign central banks stemmed the dollar's decline temporarily. The year-end 1987 budget deficit compromise and continued intervention appear to have eased some concerns and reduced pressures on the dollar. To fully restore investor confidence, however, more fundamental policy changes are needed to eliminate the budget deficit and dependence of the United States on foreign capital.

The dollar's sharp decline has finally begun to improve the competitiveness of U.S. industry, and the trade balance is responding, particularly in real terms. But currency adjustments by themselves take many years to turn around a current-dollar trade deficit and have costly effects on the efficiency of business decisions, on overall price stability, and on living standards. Moreover, reliance on currency adjustments can limit the flexibility of monetary and fiscal policy to deal with changes

---

[1] See CED policy statement <u>Toll of the Twin Deficits</u>.

BUDGET DEFICITS AND U.S. COMPETITIVENESS

At the beginning of the 1980s, the Federal Reserve adopted a restrictive monetary policy that succeeded in sharply reducing inflation. Tight credit conditions brought about the 1981-1982 recession, which broke the back of inflationary expectations. Federal fiscal policy, on the other hand, moved in an expansive direction. Taxes were cut in stages, beginning in 1981, in an attempt to encourage private saving and investment, with the ultimate objective of achieving improved growth in productivity. The tax burden declined sharply for both individuals and corporations, and the total revenues fell from 20.1 percent of the gross national product in fiscal 1981 to 18.5 percent in fiscal 1986. However, tax cuts were not successfully tied to overall spending restraint. Total outlays continued to rise as a percentage of GNP, and the budget deficit rose to record peacetime levels. Large cuts were made in nondefense discretionary spending, which declined from 5.6 to 4.1 percent of GNP; but these cuts were more than offset by the continued growth in entitlement programs and the very large increases in spending for national defense and for interest costs on the debt.

Unfortunately, the shift in tax policy has not succeeded so far in boosting private saving and investment rates. National saving (public and private) has been very weak, and large saving inflows from abroad have been necessary to prevent investment spending from collapsing.

Indeed, budget imbalances and capital inflows were the major cause of the precipitous decline in the international competitiveness of American industry in the 1981-1986 period.[a] Long-run forces, such as low private saving, had been gradually eroding the international competitiveness of U.S. industry for many years. Despite some improvement in long-run factors in the 1980s, our competitiveness position in the world was suddenly devastated by a very sharp rise in the dollar. U.S. macroeconomic policies caused real interest rates to rise relative to those abroad, and as a consequence of those yields and the relative safety of investment in the United States, foreign demand strengthened for dollars to invest here. As the dollar rose, domestic production became less competitive, and our trade balance plunged. In a very short time, the United States went from being the world's largest creditor to the world's largest debtor.

Policy makers did not anticipate this outcome. Past experience indicated that the absorption of private saving by the federal sector would crowd out private investment as the economy approached the full utilization of resources. However, the degree of international economic interdependence was underestimated. The strength of foreign saving inflows, which sustained the growth of domestic investment, albeit at a moderate rate, was not expected. Instead of hurting domestic investment, the budget deficit drove the dollar higher and crowded out some of the domestic production of goods and services that compete in international markets.

---

[a] CED estimated that about two-thirds of the rise in the U.S. trade deficit from 1981 to 1986 was caused by U.S. macroeconomic policies. For a description of the other major forces causing this decline, see Toll of the Twin Deficits, Chapter 4.

in the economic environment. To limit these costs and safeguard our future, we need to attack the fundamental causes of the trade deficit.

We need a sound strategy to deal with the economic imbalances threatening both the short-run stability and the long-run growth of the economy. The number-one priority must be to eliminate the structural component of the huge federal budget deficit. For many years, CED has advocated a long-term policy of a federal budget in surplus or at least in balance when the economy is at high employment levels. Given that the economy is now operating near the economists' definition of high employment, it is obvious that we have a long way to go to achieve even minimum standards for the structural (or noncyclical) component of the deficit. But we cannot reach our long-term budget objectives all at once. In the policy statement Fighting Federal Deficits: The Time for Hard Choices, CED called for a comprehensive program aimed at reducing the deficit on a steady, year-to-year basis, leading to a balanced budget at high employment over a five-year period.

Congress has adopted deficit targets, and at the Budget Summit held last November the Administration and Congress made some, but not enough, headway toward deficit reduction. Some observers believe that the budget deficit issue is not likely to be resolved satisfactorily without major reforms in the budget process. In CED's view, however, it is a lack of political will rather than any serious deficiencies in the budget process that stand in the way of progress on the budget deficit issue. (See "The Federal Budget Process," pages 8 and 9.)

At the end of 1987, Congress established the National Economic Commission, a bipartisan group of leading citizens charged with finding an efficient and equitable method of reducing the budget deficit. The task is formidable. Congressional reports indicate that the budget policies in place at the end of 1987 are not even sufficient to reach the Gramm-Rudman-Hollings budget targets for the current and next fiscal years.[2] According to the Congressional Budget Office (CBO), if no further policy changes are made, the budget deficit will be about $157 billion in fiscal 1988 and $176 billion in fiscal 1989, well above the deficit targets for those years. The budget deficit would be even larger, if it were not for the projected surpluses in the Social Security trust fund amounting to $37 billion in fiscal 1988 and $46 billion in fiscal 1989.

We believe this situation calls for fundamental changes in federal fiscal policy to eliminate the structural budget deficit. To do otherwise is to tell this generation of Americans it can have a free lunch at the expense of the next. Both spending cuts and tax increases will be necessary. We understand the opposition of some taxpayers to tax hikes. However, opposition to any tax increases implies either (a) that currently projected deficits are acceptable or (b) that nearly one-fifth of federal spending for national defense, nondefense discretionary programs, and entitlements such as Social Security is excessive and can be eliminated. Clearly, substantial cuts in spending must be made and the deficit reduced. But the idea that spending for all such programs should be cut by one-fifth does not reflect the will of the American people or the judgment of CED. Indeed, as we indicate later in this statement, CED believes that in certain critical areas, such as education, the federal government should invest more heavily than it does currently.

---

[2] The original Gramm-Rudman-Hollings targets for fiscal 1988 and 1989 were $108 billion and $72 billion, respectively, but these targets were raised in September 1987 to $144 billion and $136 billion.

Given these considerations, we believe the following actions are necessary.

- Congress and the Administration should adopt a package of credible spending cuts and tax increases that would eliminate the structural component of the federal budget deficit over the next four years. This can be achieved by basic and enduring deficit cuts of $40 to $50 billion a year. Deficit-reduction targets should not be fulfilled by one-time savings, asset sales, or smoke-and-mirror devices that do not amount to real cuts in federal credit demands.

- The deficit reduction will have to involve <u>both</u> expenditure restraints and revenue-increasing measures. Restrictions on spending should be broadly based, not excessively concentrated in a few areas. Means-tested federal spending benefiting the poor has been cut enough and should not be cut further for purposes of reducing the deficit. (This does not preclude savings as a result of increased efficiencies in the administering of means-tested programs.) Spending restrictions should extend to entitlement programs such as Social Security benefits for the nonpoor, as well as to discretionary spending.

- Defense spending must be adequate to meet national security needs, and taxes must be sufficient to finance it. If cuts in defense spending are made, they should be accompanied by an increased emphasis both on burden sharing by our allies and on appropriate adjustments in longer-term military programs and objectives. While cost-saving efficiencies in the management of defense expenditures should be continually sought, reductions in military spending should be based on a viable force structure and should be lasting.

- Tax increases to cut the deficit should not deter growth, productive investment, and competitiveness. Moreover, they should be linked to forceful and enduring measures of expenditure curtailment, with clear assurance that the additional revenues generated will, in fact, be devoted to deficit reduction rather than to spending.

Depending on economic conditions, it may be necessary to have an expansive <u>monetary policy</u> to counterbalance the restrictive effects of successive years of declining structural budget deficits. Indeed, a change in the monetary-fiscal policy mix is an appropriate way to reduce real interest rates and assist capital formation so long as it does not lead to excessive inflation.

Both monetary and fiscal authorities need to give much more careful attention to the impact of their policies on the <u>competitiveness</u> of U.S. industry. But changes in U.S. macroeconomic policy by themselves will not be sufficient to achieve an enduring restoration of U.S. competitiveness and a rising standard of living. Both the government and private business must also undertake longer-run measures that encourage more vigorous growth in productivity and improved international competitiveness (see Chapters 3 and 4).

THE FEDERAL BUDGET PROCESS

A strong federal budget process is essential to the effective functioning of the political and economic systems of the United States. However, as delays, political conflicts, and out-of-control deficits have come to characterize the federal budget performance, many have asked whether the process needs a major overhaul. CED's policy statement Strengthening the Federal Budget Process concluded that flaws in the budget process have not been responsible for the large federal budget deficits.

- We believe that the basic elements of the present budget process should be continued. Any structural changes that would weaken the effectiveness of the process should not be enacted.

- Greater recognition should be given to the fact that the lack of political will is both the single greatest cause of the budget deficit and the greatest obstacle to resolving it.

Moreover, important progress has been made in the federal budget process, especially in providing better information on which to base budget choices. At the same time, the process should be strengthened further, particularly to improve information and clarify concepts.

- The comprehensive unified budget concept should be supported. Social Security should not be removed from the unified budget, and activities classified as off-budget should be incorporated in the unified budget.

- Federal credit programs should be subject to most of the budget control procedures used with direct spending.

- We oppose proposals for a separate capital budget that would remove investment-type outlays from the unified budget and allow them to be financed by borrowing in the normal course of events. However, information on investment-type spending should be readily available and capital spending plans should be clearly spelled out (see page 14).

- Individual tax expenditure programs frequently are designed to serve the same purpose as spending programs while avoiding the annual appropriation process.

Accordingly, tax expenditures should be reviewed jointly with individual spending programs that serve similar purposes, whenever possible.

Certain abuses of the budget process that have become regular practice in the past several years should be eliminated.

- Congress should adopt a strict rule against extraneous legislation being included in reconciliation bills.

- Congress should also create rules that automatically put a continuing resolution into effect at the start of a fiscal year for any account which has not yet received an appropriation and that prohibit inclusion of new provisions in any continuing resolution.

The Gramm-Rudman-Hollings budget procedures, which encourage budget compromise on budget issues and attempt to enforce a specific deficit target, appear to have had some positive effects. But they too have failed to produce a solution to the budget deficit problem. This experience confirms CED's earlier conclusion that the budget deficit is more a question of political will than of procedure.

A controversial proposal to solve the problem is a constitutional amendment of some kind setting out precise budget rules. CED has studied such proposals and has come to a conclusion.

- We oppose a constitutional amendment to require a balanced budget or some other specific limitation on budget outcomes.

Many budget experts contend that proposals for constitutional amendments affecting the budget balance are not likely to be enforced and are easily circumvented and, therefore, may create disrespect for constitutional provisions. Moreover, such proposals either lack sufficient flexibility to adjust to circumstances or involve procedures that are too complex to be included in a basic document such as the U.S. Constitution.

However, increased fiscal discipline is badly needed, and all proposals to achieve it ought to be explored. Given the gravity of the budget deficit, it may be necessary, for example, to place greater reliance on deficit-reducing procedures such as the automatic continuing resolution proposal.

Foreign governments also have an important role to play in reducing the imbalance in world trade.

- The United States should urge countries with large trade surpluses to undertake policies that prudently boost their demand for imports and to reduce barriers to imports.

Finally, the United States and other industrial countries should pursue policies that help restore the economic health of the developing countries.

- Industrial countries should reduce their own barriers to imports from developing countries and should cooperate with multilateral financial institutions and other countries to improve the economic policies and reduce the debt burdens of the developing countries.*

The requirement that LDCs reform economic policies as a condition for receiving additional financial resources channelled through multilateral institutions is at least as important as the resources themselves. Such conditionality can encourage the developing countries to strengthen the private market system and, therefore, enable them to more fully realize the potential for increased production and exports.[3]

---

[3] For a detailed discussion of CED's views concerning Third World debt, see Finance and Third World Economic Growth.

---

*See memorandum by W. Bruce Thomas, page 37.

Chapter 3

ENCOURAGING PRODUCTIVITY AND ECONOMIC GROWTH: PHYSICAL CAPITAL, TECHNOLOGY, REGULATION, AND TRADE

Although the United States today enjoys a very high standard of living, the rate of growth in our productivity has been weak since the early 1970s and well below that of most other major industrial countries. From 1950 to 1973, productivity in the nonfarm business sector grew at an average annual rate of 2.3 percent; but since that time, productivity growth has averaged only about 0.8 percent. Productivity growth in the manufacturing sector has improved significantly in the 1980s, in part because of plant closings and industrial restructuring, but the overall productivity growth rate is still below its historical trend. Moreover, it has not improved enough to redress the earlier shortfall.

For most of the post-World War II period, U.S. productivity growth has also lagged well behind that of our trading partners. From 1960 to 1986, U.S. manufacturing productivity growth averaged 2.8 percent annually compared to 5.1 percent growth for the other major countries that belong to the Organization of Economic Cooperation and Development. Even in the period from 1980 to 1986, when growth in U.S. manufacturing productivity accelerated to an average annual pace of 3.6 percent, it lagged well behind the 4.2 percent average rate abroad. This relatively poor productivity performance has contributed to the decline in U.S. international competitiveness and the rising U.S. international debt. Lagging productivity growth and the long-run decline in U.S. competitiveness are interrelated, and both trends need to be reversed.

Over the long run, our standard of living depends fundamentally on the quantity and quality of our human resources, on capital investment and natural resources, on advances in technology, and on our efficiency in utilizing these resources to produce and distribute goods and services. The major part of the task of addressing these factors falls on the private sector. But public policy can play an important role by reducing barriers to efficient private-sector decisions, strengthening private-sector incentives to invest and innovate, and encouraging training and advances in knowledge. The key issue addressed in this chapter is how the public sector can contribute to improving the nation's long-run economic growth through policies encouraging investment in physical capital and technological development as well as policies influencing competitive forces at home and abroad.

ENCOURAGING INVESTMENT IN PHYSICAL CAPITAL

Investment in physical capital not only increases the productive power of workers but also provides the opportunity to introduce new technology into the production processes. Compared to other industrial countries, however, the proportion of U.S. output devoted to investment has lagged during much of the post-war period. Although broad definitions of investment that include durable consumer goods and education indicate that the rate of investment spending in the United States is only slightly below average, more conventional definitions of investment, which appear to be more directly related to productivity growth, show a substantially weaker picture in the United States. Virtually all major industrial countries with productivity growth rates that exceed the U.S. rates have substantially higher rates of conventionally defined saving and investment as a percentage of GNP. Moreover, the average age of capital goods in the U.S. industrial sector is higher than in most other large industrial countries. If the United States hopes to raise its investment to anywhere near the rates prevailing in other major industrial countries, it must eliminate the bias against saving and investment that currently exists in many of its economic policies.

Tax Policy

Government tax and spending policies significantly affect national savings. They also influence private saving and investment behavior, though the impact on private saving is generally less certain. In <u>Productivity Policy: Key to the Nation's Economic Future</u>, CED emphasized the importance of saving and investment in promoting U.S. productivity growth. A number of the recommendations made in that statement are relevant in the current situation.

- Disincentives to saving should be removed, and the bias toward consumption created by tax and public-expenditure policies eliminated wherever possible. Steps need to be taken to eliminate distortions that favor investment in types of assets unlikely to yield significant productivity improvements.

Some progress toward that objective was made by changes in U.S. tax policy enacted in the 1980s. The Economic Recovery Tax Act of 1981 reduced income tax rates significantly, and the most recent overhaul of the system, the Tax Reform Act of 1986, further reduced marginal income tax rates and significantly changed the tax structure, mainly by broadening the federal income tax base.

Thus far, however, tax reform has not succeeded in raising the aggregate saving and investment rates significantly. Nor has it succeeded in removing all tax-induced disincentives to saving and investment. Although it lowered statutory corporate tax rates, the 1986 law raises the corporate tax burden by an estimated $120 billion over a five-year period. This is because it eliminated many tax preferences, such as the investment tax credit, as part of an agreement to broaden the tax base in exchange for lower income tax rates.

The higher corporate tax burden incorporated in the 1986 act has important adverse consequences for U.S. competitiveness. Studies of comparative capital costs show the United States already had a higher cost of capital, including higher taxes on capital, than many other advanced industrial countries before the 1986 tax act. These considerations suggest that further tax reform is needed if we are to minimize the deterrents to economic growth and competitiveness arising from the tax-induced bias against saving and investment.*

As noted in Chapter 2, an effective deficit-reduction package will have to include tax increases as well as spending cuts. However, as we make these changes we must keep working to reduce the existing biases in the tax system that discourage saving and investment.

---

*See memorandum by **Philip L. Smith**, page 37.

● In order to minimize deterrents to economic efficiency and growth, new taxes should interfere as little as possible with economic choices made by individuals and institutions.[4]

New taxes should not favor one industry over another, and they should not discourage saving and investment. Such distortions in the tax system should be avoided because they impede economic efficiency and the growth of the economy. Revenue-raising potential is also an important consideration.

● Any tax proposal in the present context needs to be judged in terms of both its impact on reducing the budget deficit and its effectiveness in encouraging saving, investment, and economic growth.*

Government Regulation and the Cost of Capital

Government regulation also has an important bearing on the rate of capital formation. By influencing the rate of return, regulation may divert investment from its most productive uses. By absorbing resources that could otherwise be used for capital investment, business expenditures to comply with regulations relating to environmental protection, health, safety, and similar concerns also raise the cost of new plant and equipment. For some firms, the financial costs of meeting such social regulations are substantial.[5] The benefits derived from these regulations must be balanced against the financial costs.

Whereas properly designed regulation can contribute materially to the quality of life and the welfare of the community, improperly designed regulation can waste resources and impose unnecessary or unintended constraints on economic growth.

● Government social regulations should be subjected to cost-benefit tests on the basis of information that is relevant and reasonably attainable.

● The use of absolute regulatory requirements and direct controls should be avoided wherever possible. Appropriate regulatory goals should be pursued primarily through market-type incentives.

---

[4] This policy of tax "neutrality" was endorsed by CED in _Tax Reform for a Productive Economy_, p. 6.

[5] While costs for individual firms can be high, statistical analysis of the overall regulatory costs seem to argue that the measurable effects of such regulations on productivity growth have not been large. See CED policy statement _Productivity Policy: Key to the Nation's Economic Future_, p. 38.

---

*See memorandum by **James Q. Riordan**, page 37.

Investment in Infrastructure

Efficient investment in productive infrastructure, such as highways, bridges, airports, harbors, and water distribution systems, also makes an important contribution to long-term economic performance. Although the U.S. infrastructure as a whole is still superior to that of many other major industrial countries, signs of decay are appearing in many places. We cannot underinvest in this type of capital without undermining the performance of the economy.* As we indicated in Strengthening the Federal Budget Process: A Requirement for Effective Fiscal Control, the United States needs a clear accounting of the magnitude of the problem and assignment of responsibility.

- The President should periodically submit a capital-improvements program for the nation based on an assessment of broad national needs. This program should specify the portion of the cost that should be financed by the federal government, state and local governments, and the private sector. In presenting such a program, the

- President should make clear how the federal government's role fits into a comprehensive, long-term national strategy for maintaining and improving the country's infrastructure.

PROMOTING TECHNOLOGICAL DEVELOPMENT

Technological progress enables the economy to produce new or better products as well as existing products at lower cost. Throughout history, new technology has been a fundamental source of economic growth and rising living standards. Some economists attribute between one-third and one-half of the growth of real per capita income in the United States to technological change, a significantly greater contribution than those of capital and labor. Today, the role of technology in the functioning of the economy and in our daily lives is greater than ever before; moreover, that role is increasing.

Technological development depends on the ability of industry, educational institutions, and government to work together to create, apply, and protect technological innovation. CED addressed the issue of technological research and development in three recent policy statements: Stimulating Technological Progress, Productivity Policy: Key to the Nation's Economic Future, and Strategy for U.S. Industrial Competitiveness.

Research and Development

Technological development begins with the creation of new knowledge and new ideas, often through basic research. The government has always been the main source of funds for basic research. Individual firms often have insufficient incentive to invest in basic research because, even when its research is fruitful, a firm may not be able to capture the benefits for itself. In addition, the long lead time generally associated with the returns on basic research makes this use of funds unattractive for many corporations.

---

*See memorandum by **Donald E. Guinn**, page 37.

Although private industry, private foundations, universities, and state governments have also been an important source of research funds, there is no realistic alternative to the federal government as the primary source of funds for basic research.

- The government should adopt as a major national objective a consistently high level of support for basic research, primarily in universities. In the long run, consistent, stable financial support will provide the country with a strong base of knowledge for future economic growth and industrial innovation.

- The federal government should increase its funding of basic research even at the cost of other activities.

Technological development depends on successful commercial application of the results of basic research. However, U.S. industry has not been particularly successful in this regard relative to some of its competitors. In some areas, we lag behind our competitors in translating the fruits of our basic research into marketable technologies and products.

The primary responsibility for improving the commercial application of research falls on private industry. Government's primary role in this field is to see to it that its regulatory and tax policies are designed so as to minimize disincentives to commercial application. Furthermore, in some cases government can stimulate the application of particular research results in areas where it is directly involved with the design and financing of research, such as defense, space exploration, air traffic control, health, environmental control, and agriculture. In addition, government procurement policy in the areas of advanced technology products can be designed to hasten rapid application of government-funded research by industry.*

Intellectual Property Rights

Inadequate protection of intellectual property discourages R&D efforts and undermines technological progress. While protection in the United States through patents, copyrights, and trademarks may be adequate, new technologies and products are being rapidly diffused and the opportunities abroad for counterfeiting and pirating technology are increasing. Unfortunately, some countries provide only minimal levels or limited areas of intellectual property protection.

- The government has a responsibility to work with other industrial countries in dealing with intellectual property and should encourage, where appropriate, the establishment of effective laws to protect property rights in inventions and innovations while avoiding any improper interference in the affairs of other countries. Such laws should include the establishment of effective patent laws in developing countries.

In light of the fast pace of technological change and the rapidly increasing ability of violators to pirate technology, the Administration is pressing for minimum standards of protection in the present round of the

*See memorandum by **John Diebold**, page 38.

General Agreement on Tariffs and Trade (GATT) negotiations. The adoption by GATT of an international minimum standard and an enforcement mechanism is much desired.

PROMOTING EFFICIENCY AND COMPETITION

Depending on how regulatory goals are achieved, government regulation can either enhance or impede economic efficiency. The two types of government regulation, economic and social, focus on different objectives. During the past decade or so, we have seen increasing support for deregulation in the economic sphere. Significant scaling back has been achieved in the regulatory apparatus in such industries as transportation, telecommunications, energy, and financial services. In this process, government regulations on prices, entry and exit, and conditions of services have been deregulated with considerable success.[6]

- Government should continue economic deregulation in areas in which effective competition now exists.

Among the economic regulations, antitrust regulation occupies a special place. Historically, U.S. antitrust laws have focused on domestic market conditions. However, the increasing international competition and globalization of markets necessitates a new look at the underlying principles of antitrust laws.

- Policy makers should review current antitrust regulations, particularly in light of increased world competition, and consider modification of any laws that inhibit technological development and productivity growth rather than stimulate competitiveness in the international market.

- Government should not permit antitrust policies or other economic regulations to be used to protect individual firms from market forces when an individual firm or single industry experiences economic difficulty.

A second trend has been the vast expansion of social regulations aimed at achieving broad goals such as the reduction of pollution, the assurance of safe and healthy working conditions, the safety of consumer products, and the availability of equal employment opportunities. This expansion has been stimulated by the realization that market mechanisms cannot always be counted on to achieve social goals. However, the benefits hoped for under particular regulations have not always been realized; and in some cases, the cost of enforcing regulations has turned out to be unrealistically high and has had unintended negative side effects.

Social regulations could be improved by infusing market incentives in enforcement practices. Increased attention needs to be given to evaluating the costs and benefits of the programs and introducing flexibility in achieving stated goals.

- When policy makers want to achieve stated social regulatory goals, they should devise incentives and penalties, rather than

---

[6] See CED policy statement **Strategy for U.S. Industrial Competitiveness.**

dictate one path that industry must follow in order to comply with the regulations.

Regulatory policy should be viewed as a dynamic process in which necessary regulations are implemented and enforced in a manner that does not generate unnecessary burdens on society as a whole or create unnecessary uncertainties about future implementation. Such an approach can both achieve the desired regulatory goals of the United States and enhance the international competitiveness of U.S. industry.

INTERNATIONAL TRADE POLICY

In the postwar years, the United States has played a leading role in establishing a world trade system based on the principles of a free and open market and in ensuring that national trade policies would not degenerate into beggar-thy-neighbor protectionism. This policy made an important contribution to economic growth and development here and abroad.

But today, U.S. trade policy stands at a critical juncture. Huge trade deficits and the rising debt to foreigners are fueling protectionist sentiment, which could reverse these gains. Protectionist measures are not the answer to the current U.S. trade problems. CED has consistently opposed the maintenance of trade barriers, whether domestic or foreign. CED's basic approach to trade policy, which is discussed in the recent policy statement, Toll of the Twin Deficits, involves enforcement of existing trade laws, reducing U.S. restrictions on its exports, encouraging exports, and promoting new GATT agreements.

Enforce Existing U.S. Trade Laws

U.S. trade laws provide a number of legislative means for dealing with trade problems. Some of these laws are explicitly directed at unfair practices by foreign producers; others focus on import disruptions under special circumstances. Both types need to be enforced because the reduction of foreign unfair trade practices is essential to maintaining the necessary environment for a genuinely liberal trading system and to encouraging changes in business behavior in the direction of mutually beneficial practices.

- While pressing for stronger international rules on unfair trade practices, the U.S. government ought to continue taking action against unfair trade practices in order to relieve the suffering in the areas of the United States hardest hit by such unfair practices and to ward off rising protectionist pressures.

Congress has recently supported trade legislation, some parts of which are protectionist in character. We should reject protectionist legislation that runs counter to the maintenance of an open multilateral trade system.

- In revising domestic trade laws, the United States should be careful not to enact measures that would evoke foreign retaliation, suppress open and fair competition, or undermine multilateral trade agreements.

Reduce U.S. Government Restrictions on U.S. Exports

Some internal impediments to U.S. exports are caused by U.S. government policies and regulations. These domestic impediments take various forms, but their common characteristic is a tendency to make U.S. exporters less competitive by providing a greater advantage to foreign producers who are free from such restrictions. Most of the complaints from U.S. exporters about these domestic impediments center on U.S. export controls on high-technology goods and the Foreign Corrupt Practices Act (FCPA). In general, the U.S business community supports strong controls on high-technology exports to the Soviet bloc countries. However, we believe that in some cases these strictures can be counterproductive.

- Unilateral controls by the U.S. government and the overly strict application of controls on a broad range of products should be avoided because such controls threaten to undermine U.S. competitiveness as a producer of high-technology goods.

On the question of foreign corrupt practices, CED recognizes the importance of discouraging corruption in international business. But standards should be clear and consistent.

- The next Administration should introduce legislation to clarify ambiguities in the FCPA and should negotiate an international agreement on foreign corrupt practices that would help eliminate the competitive disadvantages imposed on U.S. companies.

Promote U.S. Exports

Although the importance of promoting exports to resolve U.S. trade problems is recognized, efforts to do so seem inadequate. Many small and medium-sized companies lack the necessary information, resources, and personnel to explore export opportunities vigorously. It is reported that a small proportion of large U.S. corporations is responsible for about 80 percent of U.S. exports. CED has encouraged private businesses to pursue aggressive marketing efforts and undertake other changes to improve their competitiveness.

Support for GATT Uruguay Round

For the longer run, a more desirable approach in trade policy would be to strengthen GATT and to negotiate a stronger multilateral agreement to reduce nontariff barriers and eliminate unfair trade practices. The Uruguay Round negotiations will be extended to cover unresolved trade barriers in such areas as agriculture, services, intellectual property rights, and high technology. It is vital that the United States play a leading role in the successful conclusion of the Uruguay Round.

- The relevance of GATT for the world trading system is now at a crossroads. The new round of GATT negotiations needs to be supported and accelerated by the United States and other member countries.

One practical step would be for the United States to push for conclusion of early agreements (prior to the formal conclusion of the Uruguay Round) in selected areas that can be implemented quickly to produce some early beneficial results.[7] An early harvest in the GATT negotiations could be a constructive interim step toward successful conclusion of the Uruguay Round.*

---

[7] See CED and Keizai Doyukai joint statement United States–Japan Trade Relations: A Critical Juncture, p. 27.

---

*See memorandum by W. Bruce Thomas, page 38.

Chapter 4

<u>ENCOURAGING PRODUCTIVITY AND ECONOMIC GROWTH:</u>
<u>HUMAN RESOURCES</u>

U.S. economic growth and competitiveness are also strongly influenced by investment in human capital. In education, labor policy, health care, retirement, and other social welfare areas, the public sector can play a key role in implementing policies that improve the nation's long-run economic health.

<u>EDUCATION</u>

Investment in human capital is among the most important contributions government can make to assure continued growth in this nation's standard of living and its leadership role in a global economy. In two recent policy statements, <u>Investing in Our Children: Business and the Public Schools</u> and <u>Children in Need: Investment Strategies for the Educationally Disadvantaged</u>, CED called attention to a number of warning signals in the public education system which indicate that current investment is not generating the needed returns, either to individuals or to society. (See "Deficiency in the Employability of America's Young People," below.) We identified some specific actions that need to be taken if the nation is to improve the outcome of its nearly $200 billion expenditure on public elementary and secondary schools.

<u>DEFICIENCY IN THE EMPLOYABILITY OF AMERICA'S YOUNG PEOPLE</u>

Employers in both large and small businesses are concerned about the lack of preparation for work among the nation's high school graduates. Too many students lack reading, writing, and mathematical skills, positive attitudes toward work, and knowledge of appropriate behavior on the job. In addition, they have not learned how to learn, solve problems, make decisions, or set priorities. Many high school graduates are virtually unemployable, even at today's minimum wage.

Well over one-quarter of the nation's youths never finish high school. Another quarter graduate without even the minimal skill requirements, and even those who go on to higher education need remedial reading and writing courses, which about two-thirds of U.S. colleges now provide.

Nearly 13 percent of all seventeen-year-olds still enrolled in school are functionally illiterate, and 44 percent are marginally literate. Among students who drop out, an estimated 60 percent are functionally illiterate.

<u>Investing in Our Children</u> mapped out a strategy for improving the employability of public school graduates through broad-scale reform of the education system. Specifically, the report recommended changes where learning actually takes place: in the individual school, the classroom, and the interaction between teacher and students. This "bottom-up" strategy views the individual school as the place for meaningful improvements in both quality and productivity.

To improve the employability of public school graduates, students must be taught the basic skills needed in a modern technological society. A key skill is the ability to work effectively in the English language, which employers cite as one of the three most important employability traits. Equally critical for instilling the positive attitudes and work habits that will lead to later employability is the so-called <u>invisible</u> <u>curriculum</u>: the messages schools send to students about the levels of behavior and achievement that are prized by the adult world. If schools tolerate excessive absenteeism, tardiness, or misbehavior, students cannot be expected to meet standards of performance or behavior either in school or as adults. Other components of this "bottom-up" strategy include improving the quality of the teacher work force, substantially reforming the vocational education system, improving education and research data collection, and promoting business-education partnerships.

<u>Investing in Our Children</u> found that preventing failure in the early years of schooling is significantly more effective, both for individuals and for the nation as a whole, than remedial measures in later grades. More resources, therefore, should be devoted to the early stages of educational development, particularly preschool programs for disadvantaged children, the elementary grades, and middle schools. Quality preschool programs are particularly cost-effective. The most recent evidence indicates that for every $1 invested in a quality program, such as the Perry Preschool model in Ypsilanti, Michigan, society will reap a substantial $6 savings.

Education for the Disadvantaged

CED's research in education has spotlighted the overriding importance to the nation's economic and social vitality of focusing reform efforts on reducing the large number of children from disadvantaged families who are not well provided for by the education system. CED's most recent education study, <u>Children in Need</u>, calls for early and sustained intervention in the lives of disadvantaged children to give them a better start in life and enable them to meet the challenges of education and work.

Immediate action is necessary to halt the continued growth of a large, permanent underclass of young people who cannot qualify for employment because they lack fundamental literacy skills and work habits. Many cannot attain an adequate living standard because they are trapped in a web of dependency and failure. Yet our schools, traditionally the pathway out of poverty, are failing to provide disadvantaged children with the skills and knowledge they need to be successful in mainstream society.

Reforms of the past five years have been targeted largely at the education system as it is now structured and have achieved only limited success. Strategies aimed at the system alone will continue to fail a substantial portion of America's children who lack the basic early preparation that would allow them to take advantage of educational opportunities. Instead, what is needed is a national commitment to helping disadvantaged children from their earliest years. Effective strategies must address the broader needs of these children, especially from prenatal care to age five, because such action is most likely to prevent later failure. Business, education, parent organizations, civic groups, and all levels of government need to work together to generate the political will to accomplish the task of preparing all our children for the future. Business in particular should take the lead in advocating a greater investment in the education of disadvantaged children because these children have no voice of their own.

Conservative estimates suggest that as many as 30 percent of all children are educationally disadvantaged because of poverty, racial discrimination, or neglect. Many of these children grow up in a deprived environment that slows their intellectual and social growth. The high rate of failure among the disadvantaged underscores the need for solutions that reach beyond the traditional boundaries of schooling to improve the environment of the child. We recommend a three-pronged approach to achieve the goal of reducing failure among disadvantaged children: (1) prevention through early intervention, (2) a fundamental restructuring of schools that serve the disadvantaged, and (3) retention programs for students at risk of dropping out and reentry programs for those who have already left the system.

- <u>Early intervention</u> calls for programs that focus on children from prenatal care through age five and on the teenagers who are at risk of premature parenthood. Programs designed to achieve the following goals would be especially beneficial: encourage pregnant teenagers to stay in school and dissuade young adolescents from becoming parents in the first place; provide prenatal and postnatal care for pregnant teens and their babies; provide parenting education for all at-risk parents; and provide quality child care and preschool programs.

- <u>School restructuring</u> requires fundamental changes in the ways schools are organized, staffed, managed, and financed. This would include smaller schools and smaller classes; school-based management with shared decision making and accountability; specialized teacher training and recruitment; support services within the schools that provide health care, counseling, and related services; increased emphasis on extracurricular activities that reinforce academic, social, and physical skills; and greater parental involvement.

- <u>Retention and reentry</u> calls for special programs to encourage at-risk high school students to stay in or return to school. These programs should include meaningful work experience that reinforces basic academic learning, alternative schools within the larger school structure, improved guidance counseling, and continuity of program design and funding.

To accomplish these goals, broader and more innovative partnerships are needed between business, educators, government and the community at the local, state, and federal levels.

Historically, the federal government has had an important role to play in targeting resources to children in need. It needs to reaffirm this long-standing commitment to ensuring the disadvantaged access to quality education. This affirmation should include both establishing and funding demonstration projects in early childhood education and dropout prevention and other programs targeted to children in need.

- The remedial reading and mathematics programs of Chapter 1 (Education Consolidation and Improvement Act of 1981) and Head Start have had demonstrable success, and federal funding of both programs should be brought up to levels sufficient to reach all eligible children.

- Federal funding of high-quality research, development, evaluation, and technical assistance is more important than ever for Chapter 1, Head Start, and related programs.

The costs of providing a quality education to all the nation's children will be high. But if the nation fails to act, the true cost to society and individuals will be far higher. More fully developing the talents of our children in need and simultaneously improving their lives are among the best investments this nation can make in its future.

Higher Education

Collegiate education is an area of relative strength in the United States. However, one special concern from the viewpoint of longer-term performance of the economy is the need to ensure an adequate supply of highly skilled workers such as scientists and engineers. The U.S. higher education system, particularly at the graduate level, is not training enough American engineers and scientists to support today's rapidly changing technology. The federal government needs to take action to remedy this situation. Where necessary, it should provide sufficient incentives to rectify shortages in scientists and engineers.

LABOR POLICY

Intense international competition has heightened the need to improve the capacity of labor markets to adapt to changing economic conditions. A relatively flexible labor market has long been an inherent strength of the United States and a source of significant competitive advantage over its chief foreign competitors. It is important to preserve and enhance that advantage at this critical juncture, wherever that can be done to the long-run benefit of both employers and employees.

In Work and Change: Labor Market Adjustment Policies in a Competitive World, CED presented a whole range of tested actions that government managers and workers can take to improve the flexibility of the U.S. work force. The following actions were among the most important actions suggested in that statement.

- Incentives for reemployment, especially through a restructuring of the unemployment insurance system

- Coordination of public-sector and private-sector resources at the state and local levels to facilitate quick and effective responses to plant closings

- Educational reform to offer the skills needed to prepare students for a changing marketplace

- Job-training programs involving local industries

Concurrently, because we recognize that management and labor are ultimately responsible for the competitiveness of U.S. business, we urge private-sector leaders to adopt the following measures:

- Improved communication between management and labor regarding the business's competitive position

- The use of flexible total compensation as a means of keeping wage and benefit costs more in line with the business's competitive position

- Voluntary, advance notification of decisions affecting jobs, particularly in the cases of plant closings, work transfers, and automation

- Support programs to help employees move to new opportunities both within the firm and outside

CED strongly believes that business should voluntarily provide as much notice as possible to employees about decisions that affect an individual's job status, such as plant closings, work transfers, or automation. However, CED is concerned about attempts to specifically legislate such notice, and opposes, in particular, language requiring advance notice regarding layoffs. These kinds of specific mandates fail to take into account either the highly diverse nature of U.S. businesses or the wide array of business circumstances that cause these actions to be taken. Such inflexible mandated notice would be especially damaging to smaller businesses, and would introduce a new rigidity at a time when the pressures of globalization and intense international competitiveness require even greater flexibility in labor markets.

HEALTH CARE

Well-targeted expenditures on health care are vital investments in human capital and thereby help improve labor productivity and economic growth. They also reflect society's desire to minimize the pain and suffering associated with illness. The extent to which these objectives are met, however, depends on how wisely those expenditures are made; and in recent years, Americans have not always spent wisely. (See "Rising Costs and Limited Access in Health Care," page 25.)

In many cases, the best way to achieve the goal of more moderate growth of health care costs while maintaining high standards of care and increasing access to services is through increased reliance on market incentives. Businesses could offer a

---

RISING COSTS AND LIMITED ACCESS IN HEALTH CARE

Since the mid-1970s, the U.S. health care system has been confronted with the problem of rapidly escalating costs, which have been an important factor in increasing labor costs and decreasing U.S. competitiveness.[a] In 1965, health care was a $42 billion-a-year industry; but by 1985, it had grown to a $425 billion industry. In that year, 10.7 percent of the nation's GNP was devoted to health care, the highest proportion in the world.[b] Part of the increase in the ratio reflects improvements in quality; and part, above average inflation for the health care industry. However, the increase also reflects the high cost of an inefficient financing system. It is important that these costs be held in check so that it does not absorb resources that could be used for greater benefit in other vital activities that improve the nation's economic health.

Despite the phenomenal growth of public- and private-sector expenditures on health care insurance, a substantial portion of the population continues to have inadequate access to health services. An estimated 35 to 37 million Americans lack the insurance coverage that facilitates access to the benefits of the health care industry.

Both government and the business sector have made useful changes in the way they purchase health care. But unless further reforms are effected, health care costs will continue to rise sharply, further limiting the availability and quality of health care as well as diverting resources from other important social and economic needs.

---

a Reforming Health Care: A Market Prescription, p. 2.
b Reforming Health Care: A Market Prescription, p. 1.

---

wider choice of health plans to workers and create incentives for them to select a cost-effective plan, reduce health care costs by improving workplace safety, stimulate employee participation in wellness programs, and help increase coverage by experimenting with programs designed to help the elderly insure themselves against any long-term care.

The public sector also has an important role to play both in encouraging private-sector actions and in correcting market outcomes deemed socially unacceptable. Government action should be concentrated in three basic areas: (1) helping to contain escalating health care costs by removing current disincentives for effective private-sector health care policies; (2) assisting the poor and elderly who are unable to purchase adequate health care coverage on their own; and (3) ensuring that the United States maintains a high quality of health care.

The government has a major role to play in encouraging cost-effective private-sector involvement in health care. Government should remove barriers to entry in the health care industry, just as it would in any other sector of the economy. It should also spurn rate controls. The rate and entry controls approach of a standard regulatory model will stifle innovation and entrench inefficiency. When appropriate, the government should endorse the use of market principles in both public- and private-sector health care programs.

- Government policies should avoid regulating the entry of new private health care providers and the supply of health care facilities.

- Government should also avoid regulating the services to be provided in benefit plans and the price of these services.

The objective of limiting government intervention and increasing reliance on market incentives is to enable the private sector to provide health care more efficiently and economically.

Nevertheless, some government action in the area of health care is necessary. Although the growth of private-sector health insurance has increased access to quality care, private markets cannot guarantee access for most of the elderly, uninsured workers, and those with insufficient resources to pay for necessary health care. The government needs to fill these gaps in health care insurance and, through Medicaid and Medicare, has done so for a substantial number of the poor and elderly. However, millions of Americans still do not have adequate coverage, and indirect subsidies that formerly financed a considerable amount of indigent care are rapidly being eroded. As the individuals who pay the employee health care bill seek lower-cost providers, they are unwilling to cover the cost of uncompensated care for indigents by paying more than the market rate for services. New, direct, and more efficient ways of subsidizing indigent care will have to be found. Furthermore, policy makers face an additional challenge in attempting to provide these subsidies by relying on market incentives rather than on rigid government controls in order to achieve the best-possible value for health care outlays.

- Government subsidies for indigent health care should be based on actual financial need, not, as they currently are, on measures of categorical groups and personal characteristics, and should be provided directly to the beneficiaries, thereby eliminating government underwriting of inefficient providers.

- The federal government should also gradually move toward a voucher system of payments for health care providers to allow those receiving subsidies to make cost-effective decisions, where feasible, about their treatment.

The adoption of these market-oriented principles will require a reform of Medicare and a broadening of the financing base for indigent care. A greater measure of protection for long-term care and catastrophic illness should also be considered in reforming Medicare.

Finally, the government has a role to play in seeing that a high quality of health care is maintained in the United States. In the past, much basic clinical R&D has been indirectly subsidized by those who paid above-market prices for routine care in teaching hospitals. Market incentives and more cost-conscious purchasing of health benefits by employees and employers may limit this source of funds. It is important, therefore, that the government support basic medical research and accelerate the marketing of new medical devices judged to be safe and effective.

- Additional funding for basic research should be made available through a system of government grants administered through the National Institutes of Health.

- The costly drug-approval process should be accelerated by allowing greater participation of scientific experts from outside government, as well as representatives of patients who may benefit from the drug, in the approval process. The current acquired immune deficiency syndrome (AIDS) epidemic gives urgency to the need for a more effective drug-approval process.

Moreover, the availability of new medical devices should be widened to allow more people access to the newest technologies:

- The review of whether a new device will be reimbursed under Medicare should be initiated prior to the completion of the Food and Drug Administration (FDA) approval process. This would avoid unnecessary delays in making these devices available to Medicare patients.

RETIREMENT POLICY

Public and private pension systems in the United States affect both the availability of domestic sources of capital and the quality of the labor force--two factors that greatly influence our international competitiveness and long-run economic growth.

Pension systems have a substantial impact on the quantity and quality of the labor force by affecting early retirement decisions. Demographic projections indicate that because of aging and retirement, there will be a shortage of skilled workers by the early part of the next century. At that time, almost one-fifth of the American population will be over the age of sixty-five. The combination of this increased elderly population and the steady drop in the U.S. birthrate since 1960 will create a dramatic rise in the proportion of nonworkers to workers if current trends continue.

The aging of the population could adversely affect future economic growth not only because of the labor shortages it will create but also because it will place a very heavy strain on the availability of domestic sources of capital. Economic growth will diminish if resources are diverted from investment to pay retirees' needs. This situation argues for policies that encourage workers to delay retirement.

It now appears that the reforms enacted in 1983 will result in large surpluses in the Social Security trust fund during the next twenty years. In fact, the latest CBO report forecasts a surplus of $37 billion in the current fiscal year and a total surplus of almost half a trillion dollars by 1993.[8] Nevertheless, the Social Security system's long-term solvency is less certain, and its current surpluses may not be sufficient to avoid real hardships and insecurity for future retirees and inequitable burdens on future working generations. Thus, our retirement system needs to be reevaluated to ensure sound practices. Given the huge current rise in the federal funds deficit (i.e., excluding Social Security funds) and the rise in our debt to foreigners, there will be substantial burdens on future generations in addition to retirement funding. Consequently, the government should strongly consider policies to increase national saving.

Those who have already retired or who are retiring now receive much more from the Social Security system than they paid into it. However, it is very likely that contributions will increase relative to benefits in future years. We believe that public and private retirement policies need to be forged to achieve two goals: (1) a minimum level of retirement income for all workers and their families and (2) an environment in which both workers and employers have the opportunity and the responsibility to meet their own retirement income goals above their minimum level of income.[9] To accomplish these goals, a three-tiered strategy should be emphasized, with Social Security providing the first tier of support, employer pension plans the second, and personal savings the third. Increased reliance on private saving is an important stimulus to private investment and long-run economic growth, and it may also reduce pressures for increased benefits from the public sector.

In Reforming Retirement Policies, CED urged broad reforms in both public and private pensions. Some, though not all, of the proposed policy changes in the Social Security system have become law. However, additional reforms are needed to improve the equity and financing of the Social Security system.

- The normal retirement age for Social Security should be raised to sixty-eight and the early retirement age to sixty-five for those who can work that long. This should be phased in gradually so that no abrupt change occurs for anyone about to retire, but it should go into effect much more promptly than is contemplated under current law.[10]

- In years when the average wage of workers rises less than the annual increase in the Consumer Price Index, the annual automatic increase in Social Security benefits should be at the same rate as the rise in average wages. Under the current law, average wages are employed for indexing only when the combined

---

[8] Congressional Budget Office, The Economic and Budget Outlook (Washington, D.C.: U.S. Government Printing Office, February 1988), p. 77.

[9] See CED policy statement Reforming Retirement Policies, p. 5.

[10] The present law provides for a gradual raise in the regular retirement age beginning in the year 2000, eventually reaching sixty-seven in the year 2027.

assets of the Social Security retirement and disability trust funds fall below a specified percentage of annual outlays.

- Fifty percent of all Social Security benefits should be taxed. Currently, 50 percent of benefits are taxed only when the taxpayer's combined income exceeds a $25,000 threshold for a single return and $32,000 for a joint return.

Now that the tax law has been reformed, the elderly poor are exempt from income taxation by more generous personal exemptions, the regular standard deductions, and special deductions for the elderly. CBO has estimated that if the thresholds were eliminated, these provisions in the income tax code would still exclude 46 percent of recipient households from having to pay any tax on Social Security benefits.[11]

Employer pension plans should provide the second tier of retirement income. To accomplish this, policies need to be developed to increase the coverage and flexibility of these plans. The private sector must take the lead in expanding these plans and designing them to take the capabilities and interests of older workers into account, but public-sector policies can strengthen this tier as well:

- Changes in the tax laws and regulatory policy should make it more attractive for employers to establish pension plans.

In addition, the government might consider requiring employers who do not have an employer-based pension plan to establish a 401K plan and provide payroll deductions if a majority of the employees voted for establishing such a plan.

To ensure that older workers and retirees can lead full and meaningful lives:

- Any existing regulations and labor market policies that inhibit flexibility in work arrangements for older workers should be removed.

The third source of retirement income, personal savings, has been greatly neglected and we urge that more attention be focused on both private and public actions that encourage private saving.

---

[11] Congressional Budget Office, Reducing the Deficit: Spending and Revenue Options (Washington, D.C.: U.S. Government Printing Office, March 1988), p. 326.

Chapter 5

IMPROVING THE PERFORMANCE OF THE PUBLIC SECTOR

For many years, CED has had an interest in improving the management of federal, state, and local governments and has published several policy statements on this subject.[12]   In this chapter, we briefly review those management issues of interest to the next President and to state and local officials.   We also address economic policies at the state and local levels which have important implications for the vitality of the U.S. economy as a whole.

MANAGEMENT IN GOVERNMENT

The policies recommended for the federal government in Chapters 2, 3, and 4 will not achieve their objectives if they are not managed skillfully.   At the heart of efforts to improve the government's efficiency and effectiveness are the capability and motivation of federal personnel.   No President, even with the support of an extensive White House and Executive Office staff, can expect to manage the massive and complex federal establishment without winning the loyalty and fully utilizing the talents of the men and women in public service.[13]   Although reforms in the civil service system have been adopted in recent years, greater efforts are needed to achieve a closer relationship between pay and performance and to evaluate those reforms already put in place.

As the federal government has cut back on grants to state and local governments, the initiative for many domestic policies has shifted to the state-local sector.   This shift makes it all the more important that state and local governments achieve the highest-possible degree of professionalism in government policy and management.   In anticipation of this shift, the CED policy statement, Improving Productivity in State and Local Government, calls for the adoption of new approaches to the delivery of public services.   It stresses the importance of better management, strengthening the work force, the improved application of capital and technology, and more effective use of the private sector to provide public services.   Although improvements have been made recently in many of these areas, there is a new appreciation of the need for improving the effectiveness and efficiency of increasingly burdened state and local governments.   In Improving Management of the Public Work Force: The Challenge to State and Local Government, CED has called attention to the importance of human resources in the delivery of public services.

---

[12] CED has also addressed problems in the legislative process and made numerous proposals for reforming the federal budget process.   (See "The Federal Budget Process," pages 8 and 9 in this statement.)

[13] See CED Program Statement Revitalizing the Federal Personnel System.

It is apparent, however, that state and local governments cannot handle the increased load alone. They need the involvement of the private sector. In CED's policy statement <u>Public-Private Partnership: An Opportunity for Urban Communities</u> we have outlined an agenda that would enable government, business, neighborhoods, and nonprofit organizations to work together to address problems of mutual interest. Considerable progress has been made already in developing a wide range of public-private partnerships at the state and local levels throughout the United States.

In fact, it is at the state and local levels that some of the most imaginative public policies and private-sector initiatives have occurred in the past decade. The challenge today is to build on that experience and redouble those efforts in bracing for the even greater challenge that confronts state and local governments in the future.

Many of the policies recommended in this report will require action by state governments. These include:

- Investing in primary and secondary education

- Preventing and remedying the problems of the educationally disadvantaged

- Stressing reemployment in the Unemployment Insurance program

- Assisting dislocated workers in adjusting to new jobs

- Strengthening technology and the links between university and business

- Promoting exports on the part of small and medium-sized businesses

This wide range of state involvement in key public policy issues is a reflection of the substantial powers that reside at the state level. Over the past decade, states have begun to exercise these powers in innovative ways. In a sense, they have become the policy leaders on key issues facing the country. In no area is this more the case than in economic policy.

ECONOMIC POLICIES OF STATE AND LOCAL GOVERNMENTS

CED studies have highlighted the critical role that state and local governments play in the health of the economy. Local governments provide basic services--such as education, infrastructure, and natural resource management--that are important to the economic health of the private sector. State governments are the link in economic federalism, often implementing and managing federal policies. State governments also satisfy a need for experimentation with different government policy approaches. When the experiments work, other states and the federal government can adopt their approaches. When the experiments fail, instructive experience has been gained without damaging the whole economy.

● The federal government should be careful that its policies do not stifle such creativity at the state and local levels.

In regard to economic development, successful states no longer focus exclusively or even principally on recruiting outside businesses to locate in the state. Instead, they focus most of their energies on providing the appropriate environment for fostering development from within the state. In Leadership for Dynamic State Economies, we describe a strategy for state governments to encourage economic growth from within.

● The key to economic vitality is a dynamic, market-driven private sector. State governments need to assure that their policies facilitate change and support innovation in the private sector.

● States need a broadly conceived strategy to identify priority actions, to give cohesion to government actions, and to avoid actions that may be harmful to the economy.

● Economic strategy for the states has these components: (1) diagnosis of the state's economic potential and evaluation of current policies in the light of changing economic conditions; (2) vision to see the policies needed to create a climate conducive to entrepreneurship; and (3) actions that are specific, timely, and accountable.

The key ingredients needed to implement institutional action are: (1) leadership from all sectors (including government, business, labor, universities) to direct individual institutions toward productive economic actions and (2) partnerships among institutions in the public and private sectors to link common interests and mobilize resources to the benefit of the state economy as a whole.

In Public-Private Partnership: An Opportunity for Urban Communities, CED points out that public-private cooperation has great potential for development in urban communities. Local governments should initiate and encourage public-private joint ventures and private activity for the public benefit. Individual and corporate involvement and leadership can be sources of energy and vitality in urban America.

Chapter 6

DOMESTIC ECONOMIC POLICIES AND U.S. LEADERSHIP

The goal of the policies recommended in this statement is to improve economic growth, stability, and competitiveness in the United States. A healthy, growing economy is necessary both to improve economic conditions for our citizens and to enable the United States to maintain its leadership position in the world.

Without sufficient growth, we will not have the resources to improve the quality of life for our children. Although Americans take great pride in the fact that their standard of living is one of the world's highest, in some ways their quality of life still does not measure up. Our average life expectancy is lower than that in twelve other countries; our rate of infant mortality is worse than in thirteen other countries; our standards of education and literacy lag behind those of a number of other advanced countries; and major crimes are more prevalent here than in many other countries.[14] Recent data indicate that except in the case of the elderly, we have made no progress in reducing the proportion of people living below the poverty level during the last decade. Indeed, about one child in five American children today is born into poverty.

It is widely understood that a healthy economy is a precondition for improving social conditions at home, but it has only recently been recognized that a dynamic domestic economy also plays a role in U.S. leadership abroad.

THE U.S. LEADERSHIP ROLE IN THE WORLD

For most of this century, the United States has been the leader of the free world. It has worked continuously for economic progress at home and abroad, often going out of its way to help other countries as part of a broad conception of its self-interest. After World War II, this country strongly promoted economic recovery of the nations devastated by war. Since that time, it has frequently used its influence to encourage political freedom, military security, and the economic development of both the advanced and the developing countries.

U.S. international leadership is as necessary today as it was in the past. It is needed to encourage the nations of the world to take advantage of the new opportunities for prosperity that are presented by new technology and efficient economic organization. It is also needed to counter the many dangerous forces that appear to be on the rise in the world and would undermine progress already

---

[14] World Resources Institute and The International Institute for Environment and Development, World Resources 1986: An Assessment of the Resource Base that Supports the Global Economy (New York: Basic Books, Inc., 1986), pp. 238-239, 242-243.

achieved. These forces include mercantilistic tendencies that threaten free trade; international drug traffic and crime that threaten our security and well-being; political repression and armed insurgencies that threaten freedom in many places; and violent terrorism that generates fear and undermines constructive resolution of problems. Leadership from the United States is needed to organize effective opposition to these dangerous trends.

However, the U.S. role as an international leader requires a different approach in today's world. The other major industrial nations have grown to positions of economic strength and influence that should be taken into account. Rapidly developing nations now have a significant impact in many markets. And the rising populations elsewhere in the world, now dwarfing our own, are pressing for more consideration. The significance of all these changes is magnified by the much greater international economic interdependence being created by the progressive globalization of markets for financial assets, goods, services, and technology.

This kind of world calls for a higher ratio of consensus building to unilateral action, of mutual cooperation in contrast with go-it-alone or do-it-my-way policies, at least among friendly nations. Even when it is impossible or very time-consuming to reach a consensus, the impact of interim unilateral national action on friendly nations must be taken into account, and the feedback from such action must be considered.

To be an effective world leader in this changed environment, a nation must: (1) provide an example at home; (2) have a realistic vision for its own development and of the world; (3) have resources sufficient to generate forward momentum; and (4) have the desire and ability to act in pursuit of its vision. Clearly, the United States still has the potential resources needed for such leadership. But in some respects, we have not managed our resources well. Our budget and trade deficits, as well as certain pressing social problems, suggest that we have not kept our own house in order. It is difficult to be a poor performer at home and the world's largest debtor and at the same time lead others to appropriate economic and political behavior. But our international leadership position can be buttressed if our political leaders demonstrate the ability and will to act in timely fashion to deal with our major domestic problems.

BUILDING A CONSENSUS FOR ACTION

For several years, the U.S. political system has been very slow to act on several issues that are basic to the welfare of our society. This seeming inability to come quickly to grips with important domestic policy problems such as the federal deficit and the festering social problems of poverty, drugs, and crime is damaging our economy, our quality of life, and our ability to lead other nations toward a better life. Such key inadequacies are detracting from the successes we have achieved in other respects. It is time for the United States to demonstrate--to itself and to the world--a more effective ability to deal with these problems.

In part, the paralysis of the political system on these issues reflects its great sensitivity to the wishes of many diverse groups in our society. However, some special-interest groups have narrow objectives and successfully block progress in

35

other areas. Others have deeply held ideological views that magnify differences far beyond their practical importance. What is needed in this environment is strong political leadership to develop a consensus for action. Timely political compromise to achieve a working consensus dealing with key domestic issues is needed before the problems become much worse and much more costly to cure. Only in this way can the United States resolve its problems and retain its critical role as the leader of the free world.

36

SELECTED BIBLIOGRAPHY OF CED STATEMENTS

Children In Need: Investment Strategies for the Educationally Disadvantaged, 1987

Finance and Third World Economic Growth, 1987

Fighting Federal Deficits: The Time for Hard Choices, 1984

Improving Management of the Public Work Force: The Challenge to State and Local Government, 1978

Improving Productivity in State and Local Government, 1976

Investing in Our Children: Business and the Public Schools, 1985

Productivity Policy: Key to the Nation's Economic Future, 1983

Public-Private Partnership: An Opportunity for Urban Communities, 1982

Reforming Health Care: A Market Prescription, 1987

Reforming Retirement Policies, 1981

Revitalizing the Federal Personnel System, 1978

Stimulating Technological Progress, 1980

Strategy for U.S. Industrial Competitiveness, 1984

Strengthening the Federal Budget Process: A Requirement for Effective Fiscal Control, 1983

Tax Reform for a Productive Economy, 1985

Toll of the Twin Deficits, 1987

United States-Japan Trade Relations: A Critical Juncture, 1987

Work and Change: Labor Market Adjustment Policies in a Competitive World, 1987

BIBLIOGRAPHY OF OTHER PUBLICATIONS

The Economic and Budget Outlook. Congressional Budget Office, Washington, D.C.: U.S. Government Printing Office, 1988

Reducing the Deficit: Spending and Revenue Options. Congressional Budget Office, Washington, D.C.: U.S. Government Printing Office, 1988

World Resources 1986: An Assessment of the Resource Base that Supports the Global Economy. World Resources Institute and The International Institute for Environment and Development. New York: Basic Books, Inc., 1986

MEMORANDA OF COMMENT, RESERVATION, OR DISSENT

Page 10, by **W. Bruce Thomas**

The United States currently imports over 60 percent of total LDC exports of manufactured goods. Japan and the EC must be encouraged to take a larger share of these exports.

Page 12, by **Philip L. Smith**

I continue to believe that the federal deficit should require further reductions in federal spending. However, should the time come when federal spending is clearly declining as a per cent of GNP and additional revenues must be raised to close the gap further, a temporary, declining income tax surcharge would seem appropriate. Such a surcharge, superimposed on the more level playing field established by the 1986 Tax Reform Law, appears to represent the fairest, least disruptive approach for our economy and one that should achieve a balanced budget within a reasonable amount of time.

Page 13, by **James Q. Riordan,** with which **Roderick M. Hills** and **W. Bruce Thomas** have asked to be associated

The report correctly emphasizes (1) that we need to eliminate disincentives to savings and investment and (2) that any new tax proposals should be judged not only in terms of their hoped-for impact on the deficit but also on their effectiveness in promoting savings, investment and growth.

Unfortunately, the U.S. income tax law (a) imposes a double tax on corporate earnings, (whereas many other industrialized nations have systems for ameliorating such double taxation); (b) burdens foreign investment by U.S. companies more heavily than the systems of other industrialized nations and (c) permits slower capital recovery than do our competitors.

The 1986 Tax Reform Act paid for the welcomed lowering of income tax rates by increasing the tax on corporations and increasing the disincentives for investment here and abroad. If we were to again increase corporate income taxes in an attempt to reduce the deficit we would further discourage savings, investment and growth. New taxes if needed should be imposed on consumption.

Page 14, by **Donald E. Guinn,** with which **Philip A. Campbell** has asked to be associated

The national set of telecommunications networks forms as vital a part of the productive infrastructure as transportation and water systems, and should be acknowledged as such when developing economic policy. In fact, our economic dependence on telecommunications is increasing rapidly; our society becomes more information-oriented by the day, propelled by rapid change in the ability of computers to communicate with each other over telephone networks. While recent changes in telecommunications industry structure have stimulated growth and innovation in some types of network services, the complex web of current state and federal policies -- legislative, regulatory and judicial -- do not provide coherent incentives for broad scale network investment or technology development. Meanwhile, several of our largest international competitors have targeted the telecommunications sector as critical to their national economic development and have already instituted policies which highlight its importance. All U.S. efforts to conserve and promote our economic infrastructure must therefore include a more coherent set of policies designed to foster investment in the capabilities of our telecommunications networks, for the future benefit and security of all elements in our society.

Page 15, by **John Diebold**, with which **William F. May** has asked to be associated

In any consideration of technology and public policy, I believe that attention should be given to the potential role of privatization in the delivery of public services. By creating a domestic market for societal infrastructure systems, private investment will be forthcoming for the development of technology based services. This is precisely the kind of commercial market technology with high export potential which we need to encourage and which we have consistently shown little interest in funding publicly. These services are today almost entirely labor rather than capital or technology intensive. Efforts to push the use of technology in these areas have consistently been about as effective as pushing a string. It is my belief that if a demand pull could be created via the profit incentive, substantial additional private investment would be applied to R&D as well as facilities in the many large societal infrastructure projects that will inevitably represent a large part of the worldwide application of technology in the years ahead.

Technology suitable for such uses as: road as well as air traffic control; community security and fire detection; and education and medical service delivery, will represent an increasing portion of world technology markets. By focusing on the creation of domestic markets in these areas, through privatization, rather than relying on government expenditures, there is a considerable opportunity for the development of proprietary U.S. technology with sizable markets abroad.

This is only one of several areas in which attention to the changes in institutional relationships and processes in the public/private interface deserves attention as a means of materially benefitting U.S. international competitiveness.

Page 19, by **W. Bruce Thomas**

If the recommended trade-related actions all take place and the U.S. merchandise trade and current account deficit continue at unreasonable levels, the approach suggested by former Secretaries Vance and Kissinger in their recently published, "An Agenda for 1989," should be considered. They recommend that in the case of Japan, "The American-Japanese dialogue must not be confined to mutual harassment. The two countries should seek to establish overall goals and work toward them. One step would be to establish an overall trade balance the United States would find tolerable; within that balance, Japan would have the choice of either reducing its exports or increasing its imports, thus removing the need for sector-by-sector industrial negotiations."

OBJECTIVES OF THE COMMITTEE FOR ECONOMIC DEVELOPMENT

For over forty years, the Committee for Economic Development has been a respected influence on the formation of business and public policy. CED is devoted to these two objectives:

To develop, through objective research and informed discussion, findings and recommendations for private and public policy that will contribute to preserving and strengthening our free society, achieving steady economic growth at high employment and reasonably stable prices, increasing productivity and living standards, providing greater and more equal opportunity for every citizen, and improving the quality of life for all.

To bring about increasing understanding by present and future leaders in business, government, and education, and among concerned citizens, of the importance of these objectives and the ways in which they can be achieved.

CED's work is supported strictly by private voluntary contributions from business and industry, foundations, and individuals. It is independent, nonprofit, nonpartisan, and nonpolitical.

The 225 trustees, who generally are presidents or board chairmen of corporations and presidents of universities, are chosen for their individual capacities rather than as representatives of any particular interests. By working with scholars, they unite business judgment and experience with scholarship in analyzing the issues and developing recommendations to resolve the economic problems that constantly arise in a dynamic and democratic society.

Through this business-academic partnership, CED endeavors to develop policy statements and other research materials that commend themselves as guides to public and business policy; that can be used as texts in college economics and political science courses and in management training courses; that will be considered and discussed by newspaper and magazine editors, columnists, and commentators; and that are distributed abroad to promote better understanding of the American economic system.

CED believes that by enabling business leaders to demonstrate constructively their concern for the general welfare, it is helping business to earn and maintain the national and community respect essential to the successful functioning of the free enterprise capitalist system.

42

CED HONORARY TRUSTEES

44

RESEARCH ADVISORY BOARD

CED COUNTERPART ORGANIZATIONS
IN FOREIGN COUNTRIES

Close relations exist between the Committee for Economic Development and independent, nonpolitical research organizations in other countries. Such counterpart groups are composed of business executives and scholars and have objectives similar to those of CED, which they pursue by similarly objective methods. CED cooperates with these organizations on research and study projects of common interest to the various countries concerned. This program has resulted in a number of joint policy statements involving such international matters as energy, East-West trade, assistance to developing countries, and the reduction of nontariff barriers to trade.

CE	Círculo de Empresarios Serrano Jover 5-2°, 28015 Madrid, Spain
CEDA	Committee for Economic Development of Australia GPO Box 2117T Melbourne 3001, Australia
CEPES	Vereinigung für Wirtschaftlichen Fortschritt e.v. Weissfrauenstrasse 9 6000 Frankfurt a. M. II, West Germany
IDEP	Institut de l'Entreprise 6, rue Clément Marot, 75008 Paris, France
経済同友会	Keizai Doyukai (Japan Association of Corporate Executives) Japan Industry Club Bldg. 1-4-6 Marunouchi, Chiyoda-ku, Tokyo 100, Japan
PSI	Policy Studies Institute 100 Park Village East, London NW1 3SR, England
SNS	Studieförbundet Näringsliv och Samhälle (Center for Business and Policy Studies) Sköldungagatan 2, S 11427 Stockholm, Sweden

COMMITTEE FOR ECONOMIC DEVELOPMENT
477 MADISON AVENUE, NEW YORK, NY 10022

COMMITTEE FOR ECONOMIC DEVELOPMENT
477 MADISON AVENUE, NEW YORK, NY 10022